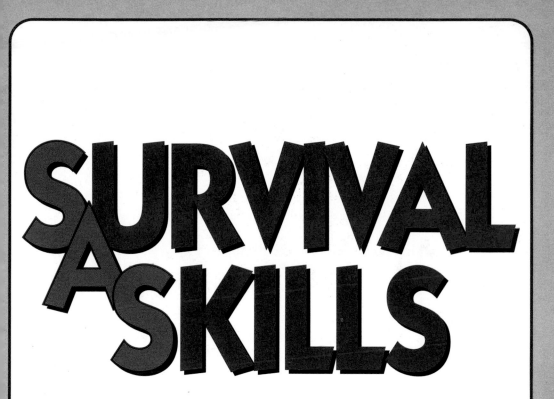

SURVIVAL SKILLS

The Diagram Group

SAS Survival Skills

© Diagram Visual Information Ltd. 1997
  195 Kentish Town Road
  London
  NW5 2JU

First published in Great Britain in 1997 by
Brockhampton Press Ltd
20 Bloomsbury Street
London
WC1 2QA
a member of the Hodder Headline Group PLC

ISBN 1-86019-814-7

Also in this series:
Boxing Skills
Calligraphy
Card Games
Chinese Astrology
Drawing People
How the Body Works
Identifying Architecture
Kings and Queens of Britain
Magic Tricks
Origami
Party Games
Pub Games
Soccer Skills
Understanding Heraldry
World History

Introduction

In any emergency you are unlikely to have time to refer to a book so it is essential that you know what to do before disaster strikes.

This guide gives useful tips on how to survive and how to improvise when the right materials are not available. Above all, don't panic, and use the knowledge acquired from this book.

Contents

Finding your way in the wild

HOW TO USE A MAP AND COMPASS
Finding out where you are on a map

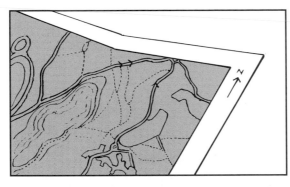

1 Find the arrows on the map which identify north. Some maps have two arrows, one showing true north and one showing magnetic north.

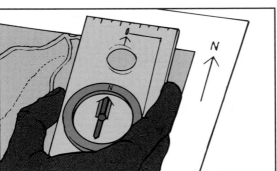

2 Put your compass on the map. Turn the map (not the compass) until the arrows pointing north and the magnetic compass needle are aligned.

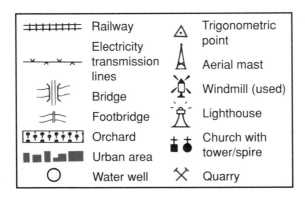

┼┼┼┼┼┼┼	Railway	△	Trigonometric point
─×─×─×─	Electricity transmission lines	⚊	Aerial mast
╣╟	Bridge	Windmill (used)
╪	Footbridge	Lighthouse
🌱🌱🌱🌱	Orchard	♦♦	Church with tower/spire
▪▫▪▪	Urban area		
○	Water well	✕	Quarry

3 Look around for a clear landmark such as a river, peak or church. These will be marked on the map in symbol form. Some common map symbols are shown here.

4 Align the straight edge of something such as a postcard or cigarette packet with your landmark and its symbol on the map. Do this by moving the straight edge but without moving the map.

5 Draw a line along the straight edge that aligns the landmark as you see it and the landmark on the map.

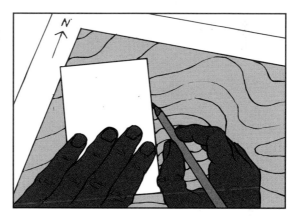

6 Repeat this technique using a second feature. Your position is approximately where the two lines meet on the map. It is always a good idea to pick a third landmark and double check.

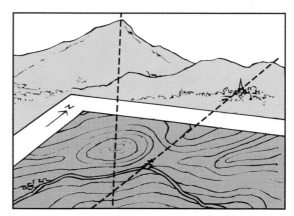

HOW TO FIND NORTH USING A WATCH

1 Hold your watch face up. Turn it so that the hour representing local time points in the direction of the sun.

2 Next, divide the angle between the hour hand and 12 o'clock with an imaginary line. This line will point due south in the Northern Hemisphere and due north in the Southern Hemisphere. In early morning or late evening this method is less accurate.

N (Southern Hemisphere)
S (Northern Hemisphere)

N (Northern Hemisphere)
S (Southern Hemisphere)

FINDING YOUR WAY USING THE STARS

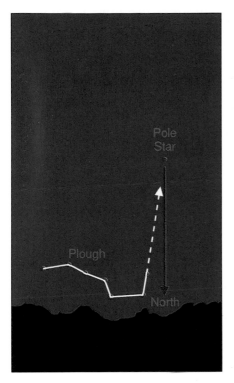

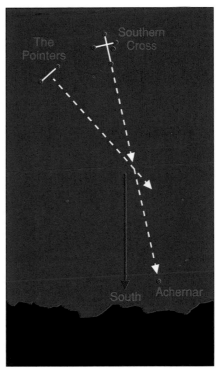

How to find north using stars

First, look for a group of stars called the Plough. Remember that the Plough may be at any position in the sky and it may take you some time to recognize it. The end stars of the Plough point to the Pole Star which marks true north. Don't worry if you can't see it at first; it is a relatively faint star.

How to find south using stars

First, look for a group of stars called the Southern Cross. Draw a line through the cross that is three times its length. You should find that due south is slightly to the left of your line, at the bottom. To check that you have the correct point, search also for Achernar and another pair of stars called the Pointers.

HOW TO TELL THE TIME BY THE SUN

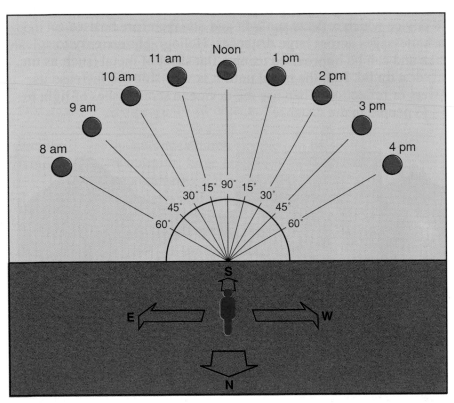

At noon the sun is due south of an observer in the Northern Hemisphere (due north of an observer in the Southern Hemisphere). So if you know the direction of due south you can also tell when it is noon.

The change from night to day is caused by the Earth turning upon its own axis, and so is the apparent movement of the sun across the sky from east to west. The spinning movement of the Earth is regular and the sun appears to move through 15° every hour. So, knowing that the sun is due south at noon, and that the sun is moving through 15° every hour, enables us to be able to locate roughly where the sun will be at any given time.

Surviving in the wild

MAKING A SHELTER

If you are forced to remain in the wild for any length of time it is essential that you provide yourself with some form of shelter to protect you from the elements. Look around to see what materials are available to you. Are there any caves or overhanging rocks beneath which you can shelter? Are there any fallen trees or boulders that will give some protection against the wind?

Examples

A Find a collection of rocks and add earth, mud, branches, leaves and whatever else you can find to make a shelter.

B Build a snow shelter (see page 27) or dig out snow from the base of a tree.

C Use fallen trees as temporary shelter from the wind and rain.

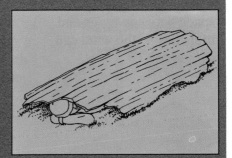

D Climb inside a piece of old tree bark.

COOKING IN THE WILD
Improvising cooking implements

Use whatever twigs and branches are around you to make spears for toasting bread or other food, for holding a pot or tin over a fire, or for making a fire fanner.

How to cook in the earth

Dig a hole and line it with large stones. Light a fire inside it. Prepare your food and when you are ready to cook it, scrape out most of the fire. Place your food on the hot stones and remaining ash. Pile the hot coals back on top and seal carefully with soil. There should not be any steam escaping. The food may take up to six or seven hours to cook, or it may take less, but once the oven is opened it cannot be sealed again so the longer you wait the better.

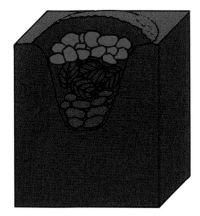

HOW TO FILTER WATER

Wherever possible water should be boiled for ten minutes to ensure that it is completely safe. Filtering water does not purify it but does improve its appearance and taste and should be done before you boil the water.

1 Find a polythene bag, a large tin, knotted shirt sleeve, canvas bag or sock. Use this as your container. You will also need some sand and some crushed burnt wood.

2 Place a layer of fine gravel in your container.

3 Gently pour in as many layers of crushed burnt wood and sand until no more will fit.

4 Make small holes in the base of the container. Pour in your water, catching it in a cup or tin.

© DIAGRAM

TESTING PLANTS FOR EDIBILITY

If you have to remain in the wild for some time and have no food it will be necessary for you to find things to eat. Plants are an obvious choice of food but many are dangerous and can cause illness and many can kill if ingested. Birds and animals are often able to eat plants that might otherwise harm a human. You must, therefore, test plants for edibility, to see if they are safe to eat. This is a time-consuming process but a necessary one.

Choose a plant. Never eat fungi unless you are absolutely sure that what you are eating is safe. Even boiling fungi does not always remove the harmful poisons they may contain. Check the stem: never choose a plant that has a milky sap as these (with the exception of the dandelion) are usually poisonous.

Once you have chosen a plant:

1 Rub some of the juices from the sap around the inside of your bottom lip. Put a fingernail-sized piece of plant on the tip of your tongue. Wait about 5 minutes. If you sense any stinging, burning or other unpleasant sensation, discard the plant. If not, continue with the test.

2 Take a piece of the plant about 2 inches square, chew and swallow it. If after two hours you feel sick or have a stomach upset, discard the plant. If not, continue with the test.

3 Take a portion of the plant about 6 inches square, chew and swallow it. If after two hours you do not feel unwell, the plant is probably safe to eat.

4 Having found a safe plant, boil it and discard the juices.

5 Boil the plant again.

TRAPPED OR LOST IN A CAVE

Trapped in a cave

If you get stuck in one of the cave's passages:

- Don't panic. Stay calm.
- Deliberately relax; let your muscles go limp.
- Use your whole body to ease yourself out. Try using your legs instead of your arms, and try moving both forwards and backwards.

Lost in a cave

- As soon as you know you are lost, stop and mark your location using a pile of small rocks, by scratching the walls or scraping the dirt.
- If there may be other people in the cave, try to attract their attention by shouting or blowing a whistle.
- Try to retrace your steps, leaving markers as you proceed.
- It is important that you make a note of how passages look from different directions; look forward and back, to help your remember tunnels.
- Try different routes, always returning to your markers. Eventually you will find the passage you are looking for.

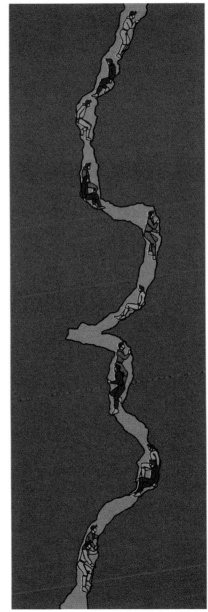

TRAPPED IN A BOG OR QUICKSAND

Both bogs and quicksand are areas of wet ground that heavy objects
sink into quickly. Bogs are found on marshes and moorlands and
are wet and spongey; quicksand consists of loose, wet sand. If you
get stuck, follow these guidelines:

- Getting out of a bog or quicksand can take a very long time and
  must not be hurried. Always remember that if you lie still you
  will float.

- Spread your arms wide and fall as gently as possible onto your
  back in order to spread your body weight.

- If you are on your own, remain on your back and search for roots
  of trees and branches to cling to. If there is nothing to grab hold
  of, remain on your back and use your arms and legs like paddles
  in a breaststroke-type movement to get to the edge of the bog or
  quicksand. All the time move *very slowly*.

- If someone attempts to pull you out they must do so using strong,
  slow movements as quick jerks will be much less effective against
  the thick bog or sand.

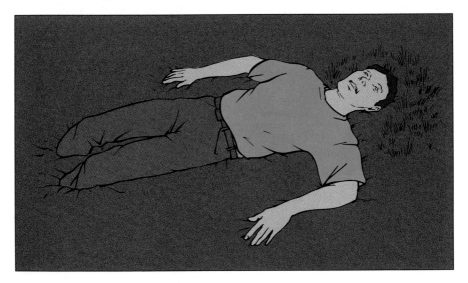

Surviving in water

SURVIVING A FLOOD

If your home is threatened by a flood, follow these guidelines:

- Turn off gas and electricity at once from the mains.

- Block all gaps under the outside doors using plastic bags filled with sand, soil or gravel, or seal gaps with clothing and blankets. If necessary, seal the outside of windows similarly.

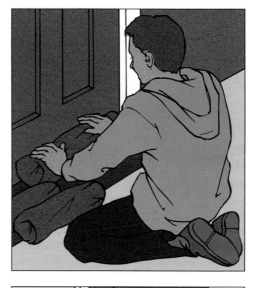

- If water continues to rise, gather together essential items (food, water, candles, matches, warm clothing and something to heat water) and take them upstairs. Also take items such as a torch, whistle and anything that might be used to make an emergency raft (such as an air bed, planks, wooden wardrobe, etc.). You may need to use rope (or sheets) to tie yourself to a chimney stack to prevent you slipping off the roof if water reaches that high.

HOW TO IMPROVISE WATERWINGS

A temporary flotation aid can be improvised in an emergency from a pair of trousers. If opportunity allows, the wings are more easily made on dry land, but it is as well to practise taking your trousers off while treading water.

1 Knot the end of each leg, and fasten the buttons or zip at the fly.
2 Hold the pants by the waistband behind your head.
3 Swing your arms quickly over and down into the water, so as to trap the maximum air inside.
4 Climb between the inflated trousers as shown.
  Reinflate as necessary.

HOW TO GET INTO A LIFEBELT

Learn this survival technique off by heart or practise in a
shallow pool.

1 Grip the near edge of the lifebelt, with your hands on top.
2 Pull the ring close to your chin, then push downward.
3 As the ring reaches a vertical position, push the bottom
  edge away.
4 As the ring falls over your head, get your arms and shoulders
  through it.

© DIAGRAM

STAYING AFLOAT

Drownproofing is a survival technique designed for good, bad and marginal floaters. It allows an exhausted swimmer to save energy and stay afloat for hours on end in warm water.

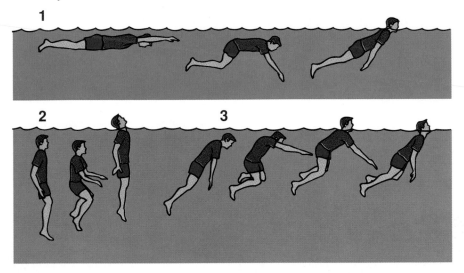

1 If you are a non-floater you need to keep moving. Stretch out flat, face down and arms over your head. Move your arms sideways and down to move forward. Drop your legs and kick. Raise your head, sweep your arms down and breathe out. Breathe in and put your face back in the water. Repeat the cycle.

2 If you float well you can rest in a vertical position, face submerged, arms and legs hanging limply. When you want to breathe, raise your arms and spread your legs. Bring your arms down and kick. Breathe out just before your reach the surface. Breathe in as you rise above the surface.

3 If you are a marginal floater rest with your back at a 45° angle. When you want to breathe stretch your arms in front of you, wrists crossed, palms outward. Open your legs ready to kick. Raise your head and begin to breathe out. Breathe in once your chin reaches the surface. You can stay on the surface by kicking gently and bringing your arms down.

HOW TO GET OUT OF A SINKING CAR

When cars sink they tend to do so engine-end first. This means that a pocket of air will form at the opposite end of the car, near the roof. It is this pocket of air that can help you escape. It is extremely difficult to open a car door underwater until the car is almost full of water and the pressure inside the car has equalized with the pressure outside.

If your car sinks:

1 Release your seat belt.

2 Turn on the headlights so that rescuers can find the car more easily.

3 Put your head into the pocket of air.

4 If there is time, close any windows or ventilation ducts.

5 Using the air pocket to breathe, wait until water fills the car before opening a door or window and swimming out.

6 It is important that as you swim to the surface you release air bubbles slowly to help equalize the pressure in your lungs.

Surviving in snow and ice

FALLING THROUGH THIN ICE

Icy water can paralyse muscles and make swimming extremely difficult. It is for this reason that it is important to try and get out of the water as soon as you can by yourself rather than waiting for rescuers.

1 Don't panic. Tread water (as though you are pedalling a bicycle) in order to stay afloat.

2 Move toward the bank by breaking the ice around you.

3 When you reach some ice that seems strong enough to hold you, try to pull yourself out. If the ice cracks, continue to break it up, always moving towards the bank.

It is essential that once you are out of the water and on firm ground that you get warm as quickly as possible. Keep moving, put on dry clothes, and if dry clothes are unavailable keep your wet ones on until you find a warm place.

HOW TO MAKE A SNOW-HOLE SHELTER

If you are stuck in a snowy region it will be necessary for you to improvise a shelter. If you have no axe or spade, use cooking pans or branches to dig at the snow.

- First, if you are going to dig into the snow in order to make a shelter it is essential that you mark your position so that rescuers can find you.

- If digging into a snow drift, start low down. Dig out a tunnel through which you can crawl.

- Next, hollow out an area that is large enough for you to sit in. If necessary, line the floor with bushy branches.

- Make a ventilation shaft by piercing the roof with a stick.

- Once inside, close the entrance. Light a candle if you have one. Wait until the weather clears or until you can move on.

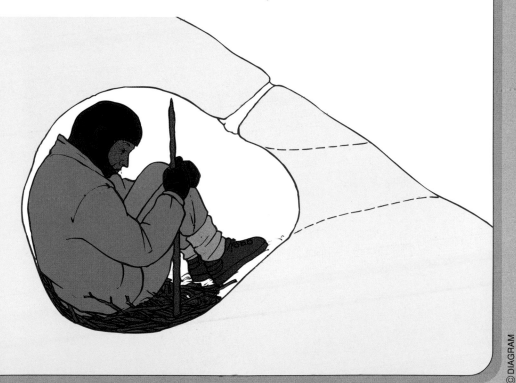

SURVIVING AN AVALANCHE

Snow sometimes hurtles down a mountainside carrying with it large blocks of snow and ice, in which case it may be moving very fast.

If you are in the path of an avalanche:

- Try to get out of the path of the avalanche by moving to the side rather than by running downhill.

- If this is not possible, remove rucksacks, skis and ski poles.

- Grab hold of the underside of a fixed object and let the avalanche pass you.

If you are engulfed by an avalanche:

- Shut your mouth and hold your breath to prevent snow entering your throat and lungs.

- Create as much breathing space as possible by wrapping your arms around your head.

- To find out which way up you are, let saliva dribble from your mouth. It will always travel toward the earth and will tell you which way up you are.

- Try to break out as soon as possible. If you are unable to break out, wait for rescuers.

TRAPPED IN A SNOWBOUND CAR

- Try to clear the snow from around the exhaust pipe otherwise fumes may enter the car when you run the engine.

- Keep the car radio or lights on for short periods only as they may drain the battery.

- Take items from the boot that might be useful, such as blankets and food. Find something with which you can make an air hole should you become completely buried.

- It is important to keep warm. Use anything you can to wrap up your body and head, including newspaper, sacking and carpets.

- It is also important that you remain awake as this lessens your chances of getting hypothermia and frostbite.

- For about ten minutes each hour run the engine and heater to keep you warm.

- If the car gets completely snow covered, use an item such as an umbrella to poke out an air channel.

- Huddle together for warmth. If there are other cars trapped, stay together for warmth in a few cars only.

- Do not drink alcohol as this encourages the loss of body heat and may make you sleepy.

© DIAGRAM

Surviving in the desert

The most important consideration if you are stranded in a desert area is to avoid dehydration.

● Find shelter. If you are in a car, use it for shade, otherwise look for trees, vegetation or rocks that might provide some shade. Keep in the shade during the day and only move about at night.

● Guard against heat stroke by covering your head and neck to keep off the sun. Use whatever materials are available to you.

● An adult can live on just four pints of water a day in the shade. Look for a natural source of water by digging in the beds of dried up streams or rivers and in damp patches at the base of plants. If necessary, collect water using a dew trap (see page 31). Drink only in the morning and evening.

● Check desert plants for edibility (see page 18).

MAKING A DEW TRAP TO COLLECT WATER

Water collects on shiny surfaces during the night in the form of dew. Wipe any water droplets from your vehicle if you have one, or use the following method:

- Find some clean, smooth stones and put them to one side.

- Dig a hole and line it with non-absorbent material such as plastic sheeting. It is best if you keep the hole shallow.

- Lay your stones in the base of the hole. During the night water will collect on the stones and drain into the sheeting.

- In the morning, remove the stones and collect the water from the sheeting. It is important that you do this early, otherwise the morning sun will evaporate the water.

- Always sterilize the water before drinking it.

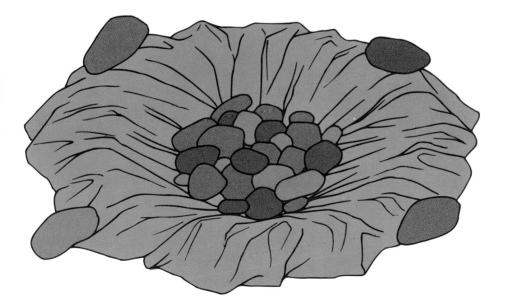

© DIAGRAM

Surviving natural disasters

SURVIVING AN EARTHQUAKE

If you are outdoors

- Keep away from anything which might collapse including trees, power lines and buildings.

- Run to an area as far away as possible from tall buildings.

- If you are in a built-up area and there is no open land, take cover in a doorway but not in cellars or subways which may cave in.

- If in an open space, lie flat.

- If you are in a car, stop and crouch below seat level.

If you are indoors

- Stay in the building.

- Take cover beneath heavy furniture such as tables and desks. If there is no furniture, stand beneath a door frame which will provide some protection.

- Stay away from windows.

SURVIVING LIGHTNING

- If swimming or in a boat, make for the shore.
- If driving, stay in your car.
- If at home, unplug the TV at the power socket and the aerial.

What to do
- Move away from high ground.
- Get away from tall trees, boulders, metal fences and other metal objects.
- Drop to the ground and lie flat.

What not to do
- Never take cover in rock overhangs, caves or in the recesses at the base of boulders.
- Never fly a kite in a thunderstorm.
- Never ride a bicycle or a horse in a thunderstorm.

Safety position
- Sit on something dry.
- Keep your feet together.
- Bring your knees to your chest and hug them.
- Tuck in your head.
- Do not use your hand to steady yourself.

© DIAGRAM

SURVIVING A VOLCANIC ERUPTION

When a volcano erupts molten lava runs down the volcano sides, the sky darkens as it fills with clouds of ash, and shattered rocks fall in the form of hail.

- Use whatever means you have to get out of the area immediately.

- Alternatively, go to the volcano shelter if there is one.

- If you find yourself faced by flowing lava, climb onto high ground.

- Remember to protect your head from flying rocks. Wear a hard hat or any form of padded headwear.

- Use any material you can find to improvise a mask against toxic fumes.

- If you have swimming goggles, put them on to protect your eyes.

- If you are in the path of a red hot cloud of dust and gases, take cover in a brick underground shelter or dive into water and hold your breath until the cloud passes.

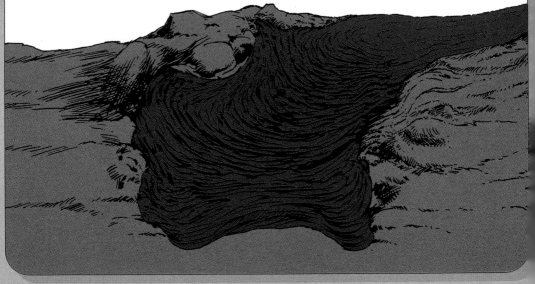

SURVIVING A HURRICANE

Hurricanes — also called typhoons and cyclones in some places — are wild storms that involve winds of up to 190mph (300km/h), strong enough to uproot trees and destroy buildings.

If you are outside

- Move away from low-lying areas, shores and rivers before the hurricane hits.

- When the hurricane strikes, lie flat on the ground and crawl to the recess of a boulder if possible. There will be a period of calm as the 'eye' of the hurricane passes. Within an hour the hurricane will resume. Stay where you are.

If you are indoors

- Lock doors and windows.

- Put a cross of tape across window panes to lessen the chance of shattered glass if they break. Stay well away from windows at all times.

- Collect together water, food and clothing and go into a cellar or under the stairs. Wait for the hurricane to pass.

SURVIVING A FOREST FIRE

- Try to get out of the path of the fire. Aim for a road, river, or anywhere where there is little vegetation, such as an area of rocks or a ploughed field.

- If you are unable to get out of the path of the fire and you are in a car, stay in it. This may be much safer than being exposed to the flames.

- If you have no car, head for the widest open area you can find. Avoid areas of dry vegetation. If there is a pond or stream, swim to the centre. Otherwise, scrape a hole in the earth and lie in it.

- Cover your entire body, including your head, with a coat or blanket.

Surviving in towns and cities

TRAPPED IN A LIFT

Lifts have automatic brakes fitted to them that prevent the lift falling out of control down a lift shaft. These brakes work even when there is a power cut.

- Stay calm. Try to help other lift passengers stay calm also.

- Summon help using the alarm button or telephone.

- If there is no alarm button or telephone, bang on the lift to attract attention, using the heel of your shoe or umbrella handle if necessary.

- Do not try to escape from the lift without help. Do not try to prise open the lift doors and do not climb out of the hatch in the lift's ceiling. If the engineer cannot get the lift working, the fire brigade will usually be called to assist.

SURVIVING A HOUSE FIRE

Finding your way out

- Aim to get to a ground floor door or window.

- Test each door before opening it. If there is smoke coming in through the door or if it is hot, do not open it. You can test metal door handles using the back of your hand to see if they are hot (**1**). If the door is cool, open it slowly, just a crack to prevent creating a draught (**2**).

- Fire is fuelled by air. Close doors and windows to prevent the spread of the fire.

- When smoke fills a room, the safest place to be is low on the ground (**3**).

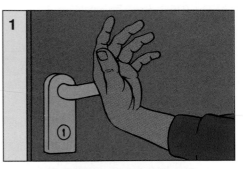

If your exit is blocked

- Head for a window or balcony. If possible, climb onto the balcony and close the window behind you.

1

- If possible, drop from the window onto soft ground such as a flowerbed.

- If the drop is too far to jump, hang out of the window, lessening the distance you may have to fall.

- Only jump out of an upstairs window as a last resort. Try to climb down from the window using knotted sheets to lower yourself (**1**).

- If there is no escape, throw water onto walls and doors between you and the fire. Cram wet rags into cracks to prevent fumes entering the room (**2**).

SURVIVING A PERSONAL ATTACK

The diagrams on these pages show some of the defence tactics that can be used against an attack either from the rear or from the front. Also shown are the most vulnerable points to aim for if attacked.

Points to aim for

Eyes
Nose
Neck

Groin

Knee

Shin
Instep

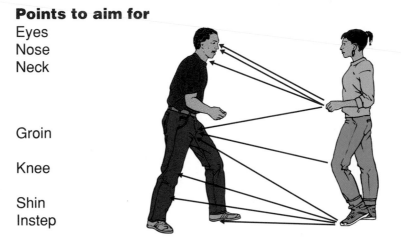

Defence tactics if approached from the rear

Hand to testicles   Foot to knee   Bend little finger outwards

Defence tactics if approached from the front

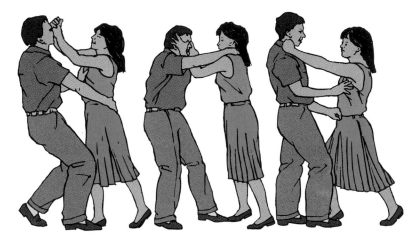

Double fist to
bridge of nose

Thumbs into
eyes

Fist to side of neck

Knee to groin   Hand to testicles   Foot to groin

©DIAGRAM

SURVIVING A TRAIN CRASH

There is usually little warning before a train crash. However, if you sense the emergency brakes going on, there are some steps you can take to improve your chances of survival.

- Your first aim is to avoid being thrown from the carriage. Stay away from windows and doors. Lie on the floor. Grab a fixed object in the carriage. Do not attempt to leave the carriage; you are safer inside as the carriage will absorb some of the crash impact.

- To help lessen your chances of getting whiplash injury, tuck your head into your chest while you brace yourself against something solid.

- One of the better places to be positioned is with your back to the engine.

- After the crash it may be necessary to break the glass of the windows if your exits are blocked. The glass is usually of double thickness and you may need to use the special red hammer kept in many carriages in order to break it.

SURVIVING A PLANE CRASH

- Follow the directions of the cabin crew; they are trained in emergency procedures.

- Remove spectacles, high heeled shoes, dentures, and sharp objects from your person.

- Make for your nearest emergency exit. Escape slides inflate as soon as the door is opened. If the cabin is filled with smoke, crawl to the exit following floor lights.

- If you crash at sea, put on your life jacket. You may need to remain in a self-inflating life raft. They are well-stocked and usually carry up to 26 people.

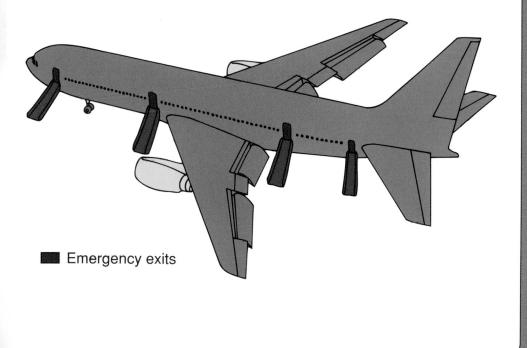

■ Emergency exits

HOW TO SIGNAL FROM GROUND TO AIR

If you have to make a crash landing or bail out from an airplane you will need to communicate with rescuers in the air. Here are some internationally recognized signals which you can trample in snow or mark out with sticks or stones, cloth or even parts of a wrecked plane. They are deliberately very simple shapes and need to be made on a large scale to be visible from the air.

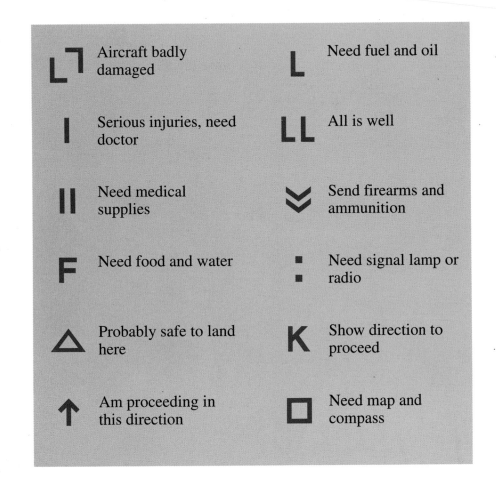

Symbol	Meaning	Symbol	Meaning
⌐⌐	Aircraft badly damaged	L	Need fuel and oil
I	Serious injuries, need doctor	LL	All is well
II	Need medical supplies	⋙	Send firearms and ammunition
F	Need food and water	⠿	Need signal lamp or radio
△	Probably safe to land here	K	Show direction to proceed
↑	Am proceeding in this direction	□	Need map and compass